I Can Talk to God

by Evelyn Kahrs

DORRANCE PUBLISHING CO., INC.
PITTSBURGH, PENNSYLVANIA 15222

The contents of this work, including, but not limited to, the accuracy of events, people, and places depicted; opinions expressed; permission to use previously published materials included; and any advice given or actions advocated are solely the responsibility of the author, who assumes all liability for said work and indemnifies the publisher against any claims stemming from publication of the work.

All Rights Reserved
Copyright © 2012 by Evelyn Kahrs

No part of this book may be reproduced or transmitted, downloaded, distributed, reverse engineered, or stored in or introduced into any information storage and retrieval system, in any form or by any means, including photocopying and recording, whether electronic or mechanical, now known or hereinafter invented without permission in writing from the publisher.

Dorrance Publishing Co., Inc.
701 Smithfield Street
Pittsburgh, PA 15222
Visit our website at www.dorrancebookstore.com

ISBN: 978-1-4349-1444-6
eISBN: 978-1-4349-1526-9

To Bob, my husband and best friend,
who supports almost all of my crazy ideas!

My mom and dad told me

God is everywhere, even inside me.

They said I can talk to God if I want.

I decided to try, and do you know what?

I **can** talk to God! I know God hears me.

God told me so.

One day when I was sitting

under a tree in my backyard, I said,

"Hey God, do you hear me?"

Then I just listened.

And guess what?

I suddenly heard God saying,

"I'm here. What do you want to tell me?"

I said, "But how do I know you're listening? Maybe you're busy with something or somebody else."

God said, "I am always with you.

I am always inside you.

All you have to do is sit still

and listen and then call me.

You will hear me in your thoughts.

You will know that I am with you.

That's how we talk to each other—

with our thoughts. Yours and mine.

You can talk to me about anything."

"Can I REALLY talk to you about anything at all?"

God said, "Yep, anything at all. I'll always listen."

"If it's my birthday and I had a great party, can I tell you about it?"

"Yep."

I said, "If my parents don't like how I'm acting, can I talk to you about it?"

"Yep."

"If I have a fight with a friend, can I talk to you about it?"

"Yep."

"If I don't like my little sister, can I talk to you about her?"

"Yep."

"If my mom and dad decide they don't want to live together anymore and we all get divorced, can I talk to you?"

"Yep."

"When I get a new puppy, can I tell you about him?"

"Yep."

"Is there anything at all, in the whole wide world, that I can't talk to you about?"

"Not one thing. I am always with you and you can always talk to me. You just be quiet and call me with your thoughts, and I'll be there to listen."

"Wow, I like that."

And God said, "I like that, too. Just give a thought any old time you want and we'll talk!"

And that's how I know I can talk to God. God told me so!